my friend is struggling with . . .

Knowing
God's
Will

**Josh McDowell
& Ed Stewart**

WORD PUBLISHING

NASHVILLE

A Thomas Nelson Company

© 2000 Josh McDowell and Ed Stewart. All rights reserved.

Scripture quotations used in this book are from the Holy Bible,
New International Version. Copyright © 1973, 1978, 1984,
International Bible Society. Used by permission of Zondervan
Bible Publishers.

Library of Congress Cataloging-in-Publication Data

McDowell, Josh.
    My friend is struggling with—knowing God's will / by
Josh McDowell and Ed Stewart.
    p. cm. — (Project 911 collection)
    Summary: Uses the story of high school seniors Doug and
Ashley, who are trying to determine what they will do after
graduation, to explore questions about knowing God's will.
    ISBN 0-8499-3798-1
    1. Youth—Religious life. 2. God—Will. 3. Christian life.
[1. Christian life.] I. Stewart, Ed. II. Title. III. Series.
    BV4531.2 .M225 2000
    248.8'3—dc21

                                     00-023364
                                            CIP

Printed in the United States of America

00 01 02 03 04 05 QDT 9 8 7 6 5 4 3 2 1

Acknowledgments

We would like to thank the following people:

David Ferguson, director of Intimate Life Ministries of Austin, Texas, has made a tremendous contribution to this collection. David's influence, along with the principles of the Intimate Life message, is felt throughout each book in this collection. David has modeled before us how to be God's comfort, support, and encouragement to others. We encourage you to take advantage of the seminars and resources that Intimate Life Ministries offers. (See pages 49–54 for more information about how this ministry can serve you.)

Dave Bellis, my (Josh) associate of twenty-three years, who labored with us to mold and

acknowledgments

shape each book in this collection. Each fictional story in all eight books of the PROJECT 911 collection was derived from the dramatic audio segments of the "Youth in Crisis Resource," which Dave personally wrote. He was also responsible for the design and coordination of the entire PROJECT 911 family of resources (see pages 55–58). We are so very grateful for Dave's talents and involvement.

Joey Paul of Word Publishing not only believed in this entire project, but also consistently championed it throughout Word.

JOSH MCDOWELL
ED STEWART

Bobby's Story

Bobby Franklin hardly noticed the cheers rising from the bleachers as he approached the plate, bat in hand. His parents were in the crowd. So was Ashley, who had been his steady girlfriend since they were both sophomores. A lot of friends from church were here too. As much as he loved these people and wanted them here, Bobby's focus was on the game. Win or lose, it was his last baseball game at Kennedy High School, and he was not about to lose his focus now. The ability to keep his head in the game and consistently make contact at the plate was a major reason why Bobby was the front-runner for the regional high-school player of the year award.

The game and the regional championship

were on the line. Digging into the batter's box, Bobby waved his bat methodically through the strike zone four or five times. He knew exactly what he had to do. With runners on first and third and only one out, he had to get the ball out of the infield. A solid single or a sacrifice fly would tie the game. An extra-base hit could possibly win the game. But a double play would end the game—and Bobby's three-year career at Kennedy—with a loss.

He will pitch you low and away; they all do, Bobby coached himself, eyeing the lanky pitcher. *Watch for a mistake, something up and on the outer edge of the plate. Then wait on it and drive it out of here.*

As the pitcher started into his motion, Bobby cocked the bat behind his ear and prayed silently, *Lord, help me do my best for You.* Bobby loved baseball, but he was also determined to use his great talent to glorify God.

The first two pitches were tempting but low and outside the strike zone, just as he'd expected. The third pitch started closer to the plate, then broke down and away. Bobby timed it and swung, fouling it back. The next one was wild, bouncing in front of the plate. Only a good stop by the catcher prevented the runner on third from attempting to score.

You're going to throw my pitch now, buddy, Bobby thought, glaring at the pitcher. *You don't want to walk me and load the bases. So you will try to hit a corner of the strike zone, the outside corner. And I'll be waiting for it.*

The pitch was outside and about belt high. Bobby kept his eye on it until the bat made contact. It was a fly ball deep to left, but was it deep enough? Sprinting toward first base, he watched the left fielder back-pedal with his focus on the ball. Rounding first, Bobby saw the ball settle into the fielder's glove for the out.

At the same instant, Mike Bryan tagged third and took off for the plate. The fielder quickly launched a rocket shot toward home. Bobby stood still to watch, wishing he had hit the ball deeper, willing Mike to beat the throw and score the tying run.

The ball and the sliding runner seemed to arrive at the plate simultaneously. Amid a cloud

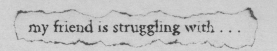

of dust, the umpire's right hand shot into the air as he bellowed, "Out!" Bobby's head dropped to his chest. The championship was lost. The season and Bobby's high-school baseball career were over.

As the opposing team leaped and cheered in jubilation, Bobby and his glum teammates lined up to offer their congratulations. "Great game, great game, great game," he said to the victors passing by, and he meant it. The stinging defeat was a disappointment. But the better team had won today, and Bobby was not about to sulk and dampen the winners' celebration.

Moments later, a sports reporter and video camera person from the local television station cornered him. The media in Bobby's hometown had touted him as a local sports hero, a title he tried to ignore. Although he'd been interviewed for the sports news a few times before, Bobby still felt uncomfortable in front of the camera.

As the camera zoomed in on him, the reporter began, "I'm standing with Bobby Franklin, Kennedy's third baseman and the favorite to win player-of-the-year honors. Bobby, you led the league in hitting and fielding. How does it feel to lose the championship after such a successful season?"

"We're disappointed to lose today. But it was a great season, and I'll never forget it."

After a few more questions about the title game, the reporter turned to Bobby's future. "There is a lot of speculation about what you plan to do next year, Bobby. Have you decided yet if you will go on to play college baseball?"

Bobby had heard questions like this a lot in the last two months. He tried not to show it, but he was struggling over his future. "I'm not sure yet," he answered, just as he had so many times before. He didn't like being "not sure," but he didn't know how to be sure about what God had in store for his future.

"You have been offered a number of baseball scholarships, right?"

"A few," Bobby corrected, "and I'm flattered by the interest shown in me. I think going to college is a good idea, if that's what I'm supposed to do." *If that's what God wants me to do,* he added silently. That was the issue for Bobby. Since trusting Christ as a child, he had tried to discover and obey God's will at every stage of his life. The obeying part had been rather simple. It was the discovering part that was often difficult. And it had never been more difficult than now, when he was about to graduate from high school and take the next step. Right now, Bobby still didn't know what that step would be.

"What about turning pro?" the reporter continued. "I know there have been major-league scouts attending your high-school games this year."

Bobby pushed up the bill of his cap and absently scratched at his forehead. The thought of playing in the majors someday had captivated him ever since Little League. Was he good enough? Would he be offered a contract? If so, was it God's will for him to sign it? Bobby didn't have a clue.

"Every kid who puts on a baseball uniform dreams of playing in the World Series some day, and I'm no exception," Bobby said with a grin. "I've seen the scouts, but they haven't talked to me yet. If they do, I'll have to think about it." He *had* been thinking about it and praying about it a lot since early spring. But, like the handful of scouts who charted his every move on the field, God hadn't talked to him yet about pro baseball.

"I hear there's a chance you may not play baseball at all next year," the reporter went on.

"It's possible," Bobby replied. "One of my options is to attend a small Bible college that has no baseball program."

"Could you really hang up your cleats after such an outstanding three years on the Kennedy diamond?"

The idea still made Bobby wince. He didn't want to quit playing baseball. But if God directed him to his church's Bible college next year, there would be no baseball. "Yes, I could give up baseball," he answered, hoping his disappointment didn't show, "if that's what God wants me to do."

The reporter thanked Bobby for the interview and then hurried off with the camera person to find the winning pitcher. Bobby's parents had been patiently waiting for him. Beaming with pride, they hugged him and congratulated him on his good game, even though the team had lost.

Then Bobby was face to face with Ashley Shepherd. He didn't know if Ashley was the girl

God had picked out for him to marry any more than he knew if he was supposed to continue to play baseball. But he definitely wanted Ashley and baseball in his life for as long as possible. As for the future, Ashley was part of the mystery God had not yet revealed to him. And since Bobby didn't know where Ashley fit into God's plans for him, he had stayed mum about their future.

Ashley gave him a hug and a kiss on the cheek. "I'm sorry you didn't win, Bobby. You played a great game. But it really doesn't matter to me because you will always be my champion."

Then, as Bobby watched, Ashley's face suddenly clouded over. She buried her face in his jersey and started crying. Surprised at Ashley's unexplained tears, Bobby just held her. *The game isn't that big a deal, so what is she crying about?* he wondered.

Ashley's Story

Ashley was embarrassed by her tears, but she couldn't stop them from flowing. It had hit her all of a sudden when the game ended: *This could be the beginning of the end for Bobby and me. In a few weeks we will graduate. Soon after that he will be off to attend Bible college or to play baseball somewhere far away. He will meet other girls and forget all about me. Then what will I do?*

Since they had started going together almost three years earlier, Ashley had just known she would marry Bobby someday. She had practiced writing the names she would use: Ashley Janine Franklin, Mrs. Robert Franklin, Mr. and Mrs. Robert Franklin, Bobby and Ashley Franklin. She had begun collecting catalogs for china, table service, and furniture and buying magazines about home decorating. She'd even made up names for the children she hoped they would have someday: Bobby Jr., Brett, Brittany, Beth.

But it was all a big secret. She'd told no one, especially not Bobby. He was so involved in his studies and baseball and the youth-group leadership at their church that he probably did not yet know they were destined to be together. It was God's will—Ashley was sure of it. They were perfect for one another. Yet Bobby had to realize it on his own.

But would he? The question had prompted Ashley's tears. What if Bobby didn't see it? What if his life centered around baseball or the ministry and he found another girl who was better suited to his career? Ashley's parents wanted her to attend the state university nearby, so if Bobby went elsewhere, she could not keep him from meeting other girls. The final out of the game had brought these fears suddenly into focus.

"Why were you crying?" Bobby said as she dabbed her eyes. They were walking to the team bus together. Bobby had to ride back to the school to shower, change into street clothes, and clean out his locker.

Ashley waved her tears away. "Nothing really, just the emotion of the big game, I guess." She felt a little guilty about being purposely vague, but she could not tell Bobby the real reason.

"I'm a little bummed myself, but it's just a game."

"You're right, it's just a game," she said, relieved that Bobby wasn't pressing her to be more specific.

"It will only take me about an hour to finish

up at school," he said as they approached the bus. Bobby's teammates and friends were swirling around them. "I can come over later, if you want."

"Yes, come over when you're done at school. My mom is working tonight. We can go get something to eat."

"Great. I'll see you in about an hour." Kissing her lightly on the forehead, he said good-bye and boarded the bus. Ashley turned away and started walking to hide another surge of tears as the bus pulled away. She would say good-bye to him again soon, she feared, only he would not be coming back.

Bobby's parents dropped Ashley off on their way home. She was relieved that the house was empty because her emotions were on edge and her mother wouldn't understand. She chided herself about being so upset. *If it's God's will for Bobby and me to be together, it will happen,* she thought, trying to be positive. *Bobby wants God's will as much as I do, so even if he goes away for college or baseball, he will still find his way back to me.*

11

Then familiar, dark questions began flitting through her mind like pesky, menacing mosquitoes, questions she had repeatedly tried to swat away over the last few months: *What if you are mistaken about God's will? How do you know for sure you and Bobby are supposed to marry someday? Where is the Bible verse that proves it? Is it God's will or wishful thinking? Is it God's will or your will?*

These questions were followed by others: *If I don't marry Bobby, what will I do? Should I start a career? Should I date other people, even though I don't want to be with anyone but Bobby? Will I end up marrying someone else, someone I don't love as much as I love Bobby?*

Ashley had no answers to these questions. How could anyone know these things for sure? Was there any way to find out? With graduation only six weeks away, the uncertainty in her heart was growing like a cancer.

Ashley was glad that her tears dried up before Bobby arrived. They went out for pizza, but Ashley didn't say much. Thankfully, she didn't have to. The pizza place was jammed with friends from their school who had already begun to forget about the lost championship. Ashley had a good time, but she asked Bobby to take her home right afterward. They kissed good night, and she hurried inside.

Another good-bye almost made her cry again. *I have to talk to somebody,* she realized. *I have to figure out how to discover God's will or I'll go crazy.* She had no idea that her boyfriend was thinking the same thoughts as he drove home.

Time Out to Consider

"How can I know God's will?" This is one of the questions students ask most frequently of Christian leaders. A lot of students have sincere, serious questions about God's will. Some talk about it, others worry about it and even lose sleep over it.

Why is God's will such a big deal for people your age? Because, like Bobby Franklin and Ashley Shepherd, you are facing the three most important decisions of your life. First is the decision about who will guide your life. As you can see, Bobby and Ashley have settled this issue. They both trust Jesus Christ as Savior and Lord. They intend to live their lives according to His Word and His will as He reveals it to them. Perhaps you have also made that decision.

The second vital decision you are facing regards marriage: *if* you will marry and *whom* you will marry. Ashley is struggling with this decision right now because she knows whom she wants to marry, but she is not sure marrying Bobby in the future is God's will. The marriage decision is doubly difficult because it requires the participation of another person. Ashley may think it is God's will for her to marry Bobby someday, but her opinion means little unless Bobby interprets God's will the same way. You may be involved in a dating relationship that is causing you to ask serious questions about God's will for marriage.

Your third most important decision centers on career. What will you do with your life? What education will you need to prepare you for this endeavor? Do you feel the pressure of making a career decision in the next few years that could impact the rest of your life? You're not alone.

If you have decided to follow Christ as Ashley and Bobby have, you have a great advantage for finding the answers to your questions about marriage and career. God loves you and has a great plan for your life. Jeremiah 29:11 states, "'I know the plans I have for you,' declares the LORD, 'plans to prosper you and not to harm you, plans to give you hope and a future.'" God also declares, "I will instruct you and teach you in the way you should go; I will counsel you and watch over you" (Ps. 32:8). All you have to do is find out what that plan is—God's will—and your worries are over.

Easier said than done, you say. Many Christian students are aware that God has a plan for their lives, but they are clueless about how to find out what that plan is. His "counsel" is available, but it is often missed, ignored, or misunderstood. Why? Because people get hung up on several wrong attitudes about God's will. Perhaps one or more of these have kept you confused about God's will concerning the important decisions of your life.

God's will is hidden and I have to find it. Some people think that discovering God's will is like hunting for Easter eggs. God hides His answers to your big questions, and if you can't find them, too bad. This attitude does not line up with God's Word. God is not playing games with you. He is eager and willing to reveal His will to you if you are willing and open to receive it.

I don't really want to know God's will because I might not like it. Some people are afraid of God's will. They think He may ask them to marry someone they don't love or spend their lives doing something they don't want to do—like become a missionary in a remote jungle. But is God a kind of kill-joy looking to make us miserable? Not according to Romans 8:32: "He who did not spare his own Son, but gave him up for us all—how will he not also, along with him, graciously give us all things?" God wants to graciously give us all things that will fulfill our deepest desires.

I only want to do part of God's will. Those with this attitude may never know God's will. It's like trying to drive a car by stepping on the gas pedal and the brake pedal at the same time. One moment we're saying, "Lord, show me Your will," and the next moment we're saying, "I don't want to do that part of Your will." If we don't follow through with what God shows us to do today, why should He show us what to do tomorrow? We must commit to doing the *whole* will of God.

I want to know God's will so I can decide whether I want to do it. Seeking God's will is not like shopping for a new car. You can't "test-drive" His will and then decide if you want to "buy" it. You either want God's will, or you don't. You will never really know God's will until you desire it more than your own.

Contrast these faulty attitudes with the appropriate attitude: *I am willing to do God's will, whatever it is.* The only attitude that will be rewarded is a willingness to accept God's will even before it is known. It is the attitude expressed by the psalmist who wrote, "I desire to do your will, O my God; your law is within my heart" (Ps. 40:8). God is eager to share His plans and counsel with those who are eager to obey.

Bobby and Ashley are headed in the right direction. Even though they are a little anxious

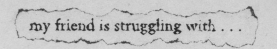

about what God may have in store for them, they are both committed to doing God's will. They just need a little help seeing His will more clearly. Such an attitude is always rewarded, as each of them will soon discover.

Bobby's Story

It was the weekend Bobby Franklin had been looking forward to. Four senior boys in the church youth group had decided to celebrate their coming graduation by backpacking into the mountains for three days of fishing and fun. Two of the guys—Blake and Ian—would be going to college out of state, and Bobby and Jeff were not sure where they would be in the fall. So they all decided to get away together before they split apart at the end of the summer.

The four seniors unanimously agreed to invite Doug Shaw to go backpacking with them. Doug and his wife, Jenny, were the volunteer youth leaders in their church. Doug, an avid outdoorsman, accepted the invitation eagerly. While Doug was in the mountains with the boys, Jenny was hosting a sleepover with several senior girls, including Ashley Shepherd.

Bobby and Doug had worked closely together during the past year while Bobby served on the youth-group leadership team. Bobby regarded Doug as a kind of spiritual big brother. Blake, Ian, and Jeff had also been helped through the friendship and guidance of Doug Shaw. Bobby knew the five of them would have a great time together. He also hoped being away with Doug for the weekend would supply opportunities to get some answers to the questions plaguing him about the future.

They left for the mountains early Friday morning, a senior day off from school. By noon they were parked at the trailhead, where they ate lunch. Then the five hikers cinched up their backpacks and headed into the woods. Shortly after 5:00, they found a campsite near a crystal-clear mountain lake. By 6:30, they had caught enough trout between them for sumptuous meal.

Sitting around a crackling fire after dinner, Doug and the four boys talked and laughed about

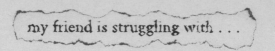

some of their high-school experiences. Much of the conversation and kidding focused on Bobby's baseball exploits, which had made him something of a celebrity in their town. Bobby took the kidding well and dished out plenty of his own.

During a momentary lull in the conversation, Bobby posed the question he had been thinking about all afternoon as they hiked. "Doug, how did you decide what your career would be, where you would go to college, stuff like that?"

Doug added another log to the fire, stirring up sparks. "You mean how did I find out what my skills were and such?"

"Yeah, but also how did you decide what to do with your skills?"

Doug smiled. "In other words, how did I discover God's will for my life when I was your age?"

Bobby felt himself blush, realizing his real question had been uncovered. "Yeah, I guess." The flickering firelight prevented his friends from seeing his face change color. Besides, Blake, Ian, and Jeff were also turned toward Doug, awaiting his reply.

Doug stirred the fire in silence for a few seconds. Then he began, "Like the four of you, I was a Christian in high school. So as I approached graduation, I was eager to find out what God wanted me to do with my life. I had always done well in technical subjects, and I had pretty good business skills. So I thought I might do something with computers—you know, sales and service or something like that."

"You own a quick-print shop," Blake put in, "so you're doing just about what you wanted to do."

"Yes, but I haven't always been in a quick-print shop," Doug explained.

Bobby realized he didn't know much about Doug's life history beyond the past three years. He was eager to hear it. "So what did you do before?" he asked. Three other heads around the fire nodded in expectation.

"I spent two years in the navy, four years in college, and seven years in my father's furniture store."

Bobby's eyes widened. "How did God get you from the navy to college to a furniture store to your quick-print shop?"

Doug smiled. "It's a long story, but I'll be glad to tell it to you. However, I want to share something with you first about God's will that I learned from my pastor when I was in high school. It really helped me get from where I was to where I am today."

With a stick, Doug drew a horizontal line in the dirt by the fire. "There are two levels of God's will. The first is God's will for everybody, or as my pastor called it, 'God's universal will.'" He tapped the space above the line. Moving the stick below the line, he said, "Then there's God's will for each individual. A lot of people want to know God's will for them individually but ignore God's universal will. That's a big problem. Why should God reveal His specific will for us if we are not obedient to His universal will?"

Blake spoke up. "What do you mean by 'God's universal will'?"

"God's clear, unmistakable will for everyone as found in the Bible," Doug answered. "For example, we know from Scripture that God's will is that everyone trust in Christ for salvation. Or think about First Thessalonians five, verse seventeen, which says, 'Pray continually.' We know it's God's will that everyone develop a consistent attitude of prayer and fellowship with Him. God reveals His will for us throughout the Bible. Maybe you guys can think of some others."

"Love one another," Bobby said.

"Love for others is clearly God's will for everyone," Doug affirmed.

"What about 'Obey your parents'?" Ian offered.

Doug nodded.

The hikers thought of several more commands from Scripture and shared them.

Then Doug said, "When I was a junior, I went to my pastor and asked him how I could tell if God wanted me to go college. He asked me if I had trusted Christ as my Savior, if I was obeying my parents, if I was staying pure sexually. I guess I looked kind of shocked at the questions. The pastor said, 'If you're not committed to obeying God's universal will, there's no point in seeking His specific will.' I never forgot that. The key to finding God's specific will for our lives is to faithfully obey what He has already given us to do."

Bobby couldn't keep from doing a little self-examination as Doug talked. Was he in line with God's universal will? He quickly admitted to himself that he was not perfect. But, yes, he was committed to obeying God's Word. He took his Christian faith seriously, even when he was tempted to rebel against his parents or compromise his sexual purity. He still had room to grow as an obedient Christian, but obedience to Christ and His Word was his top priority.

Bobby couldn't wait to hear the rest of Doug's story because it was the specifics of God's will concerning his immediate future that were foremost in his mind.

Ashley's Story

"Okay, Jenny," Ashley said, "we all want to know: How did you and Doug meet, and when did you fall in love?"

Ashley and her friends were having a great time doing makeovers and chatting. Jenny was a wonderful hostess and so much fun. Ashley loved her as a friend and respected her as a mentor in the Christian faith. The boy talk of the evening had turned to Jenny's relationship with her husband, Doug. The girls leaned in eagerly to hear her story. No one was more eager than Ashley, who could not take her mind off her uncertain future with Bobby Franklin.

"I met Doug in college," Jenny began. "I was a sophomore, and he was a freshman, right out of the navy."

"Ooo, a navy man," Ashley's friend Dana said, her voice dripping with mock passion. Everyone laughed.

Jenny went on. "Doug and I were members of a Christian outreach ministry on our campus. It was clear to me that this guy was dedicated one hundred percent to serving the Lord, just what I was looking for in a man. Besides, he was cute!" Another mischievous laugh rippled through the small group of girls.

"Was it love at first sight?" Ashley probed, trying not to sound desperate to know. "Did you know immediately that he was the one for you?"

"Not really," Jenny said. "One thing I have learned about God's will is that He usually reveals it one day at a time. I was attracted to Doug right away, and we enjoyed dating and serving Christ together on the outreach team. But it was almost two years before I was sure he was the one God had picked out for me."

"How did you know for sure?" Ashley pressed.

Jenny grinned. "Well, the short answer to that question is that he asked me to marry him at that time, and I said yes." Ashley didn't laugh with the others. She was deadly serious.

Noticing her expression, Jenny continued. "But let me tell you the whole story. During the two years we dated, I actively sought God's will for my life in four specific ways. Doug was doing the same thing, even though I didn't know it.

"First, I kept applying scriptural guidelines to our relationship. We were both Christians, so I knew we were not 'unequally yoked,' which the Bible forbids. So I determined to keep the focus of our relationship on spiritual and relational growth and avoid the temptation to get involved sexually."

"Were you a virgin when you married Doug?"

Jamie asked with a boldness that widened the eyes of her friends.

"Yes, I was a virgin," Jenny said. "It wasn't easy, but we were both committed to entering marriage sexually pure."

Ashley appreciated Jenny's openness about the pressure to compromise her morals. She and Bobby had agreed to hold each other accountable for sexual purity in their relationship. But there had been moments of closeness when she would have been tempted to cave in had Bobby pressed her. He never had.

"The second way I sought God's will was through prayer," Jenny continued. "I asked God to shut the doors to our relationship if I was not to be with Doug and to open them if our relationship pleased Him. Third, I asked for the advice and counsel of mature Christians. I wanted objective opinions about my relationship with Doug.

"Fourth, I paid attention to the circumstances that kept bringing Doug and me closer together. We both felt led to serve God with our lives, but neither of us felt called to the ministry as a vocation. We worked well together as a team. We enjoyed many of the same things. We loved being together. Since we received nothing but green lights from God for two years, we decided to go for it."

"What do you mean *you* decided?" Ashley blurted out. "Don't you mean *God* decided?"

"Actually, it was kind of a 'corporate decision,'" Jenny answered with a smile. "I knew that a relationship with Doug was in God's will, but God didn't decide for me. I had a choice in the matter, and so did Doug. God loves us so much that He wants us to enjoy the desires of our heart as long as our number one desire is to delight in Him. Had I chosen not to marry Doug, or had he chosen not to marry me, I probably would have met another Christian man who would have been just as much in God's will for my life. But Doug was the desire of my heart, so I chose him, and he chose me. And in eleven years of marriage, I've never been sorry."

Ashley didn't like what she was hearing. Next to God, Bobby was the desire of her heart. But

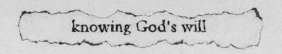

what if Bobby didn't feel the same way about her? She wanted God to make the choice—namely, choosing Bobby for her and her for Bobby. It was becoming painfully clear to Ashley that she had to talk to someone other than God about her future with Bobby Franklin, and that someone was Bobby Franklin.

Time Out to Consider

As Bobby and Ashley discovered, God's will for you is divided into two distinct categories: His universal will, which applies to everyone; and His specific will, which applies to you as an individual. Like the couple in our story, you may be more interested in the immediate specifics: What shall I do with my life and whom shall I marry? But God's universal will and specific will are closely intertwined. You really can't have one without the other.

God's universal will is clear and indisputable because it is spelled out in His Word. Let's look at several examples.

Trust Christ. The most important aspect of

God's revealed will is for everyone to be saved, to trust Christ as Savior and Lord. First Timothy 2:3–4 states: "This is good, and pleases God our Savior, who wants all men to be saved and to come to a knowledge of the truth." It's pointless to talk about any other aspect of God's will until you have fulfilled His will regarding your salvation.

Submit totally to Christ. Once you trust Christ, God's will for you is to submit your life, your future, and your will to Christ. Paul wrote, "Therefore, I urge you, brothers, in view of God's mercy, to offer your bodies as living sacrifices, holy and pleasing to God—this is your spiritual act of worship. Do not conform any longer to the pattern of this world, but be transformed by the renewing of your mind. Then you will be able to test and approve what God's will is—his good, pleasing and perfect will" (Rom. 12:1–2).

Be filled with the Spirit. Ephesians 5:17–18 states: "Therefore do not be foolish, but understand what the Lord's will is. Do not get drunk on wine, which leads to debauchery. Instead, be filled with the Spirit." The Holy Spirit entered your life at the moment of salvation. God desires to permeate your life, to control every corner of your life through His Spirit, who is already in you. It is God's will that you allow Him to fill you day by day.

Obey your parents. God's will for all students is that they live in obedience to their parents. Ephesians 6:1 is clear: "Children, obey your parents in the Lord, for this is right." One reason for this command is that God may choose to reveal His specific will to you through the counsel and example of your dad and/or mom. If you fail to obey your parents, they cannot serve as channels of God's will.

Remain sexually pure. You don't ever need to ask God if it is His will for you to become sexually involved with your boyfriend or girlfriend. God has already revealed His will on this topic: "It is God's will that you should . . . avoid sexual immorality" (1 Thess. 4:3). If you have never been sexually active, stay that way until marriage. If you have been sexually active in the past, or you are involved sexually now, determine to obey

31

God's will in this area from now on. It is God's clear will for everyone.

Share your faith. Christians need never ask God, "Should I share my faith with others?" God's will is already revealed in this area—for all believers. Jesus commanded, "Therefore go and make disciples of all nations, baptizing them in the name of the Father and of the Son and of the Holy Spirit, and teaching them to obey everything I have commanded you. And surely I am with you always, to the very end of the age" (Matthew 28:19–20). God's will is that you share your faith with *all* nations—not just those across the ocean but also with those across the hall and the lunch table.

As you set your heart to obey these and other facets of God's clearly revealed will in Scripture, you are in the perfect spot to discover God's specific will for your life. It doesn't matter which question you are asking right now: Whom should I date or marry? What school should I attend? What major should I declare? What classes should I take? What career should I prepare for? Or any of dozens of other seemingly important and urgent decisions you may face. By committing yourself to follow God's universal will, you open the door for God to reveal His specific will for your life.

As Jenny suggested to Ashley, it is important to understand that God most often reveals His specific will a day at a time. Many Christians pray, "What is Your will for me for next month, next year, or *for my life?*" But God seldom works that way. In John 16:12, Jesus told His disciples, "I have much more to say to you, more than you can now bear." If God told you what you would be doing fifteen years from now, it might blow you away. So He unfolds His will a step at a time or a day at a time so we can "bear it."

Here is a process to help you make right moral choices in conformity with God's universal will. We call it the 4C Process. Suppose a teacher asks you if you have completed a reading assignment. Saying no will hurt your grade, but you have barely begun the reading. What do you say? Or imagine that a friend tells you some juicy gossip about one of the families in your church, and you are just itching to pass it on to someone

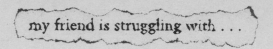

else? What should you do? The 4C Process will help you decide God's will in such situations.

C1. *Consider the choice.* Every one of these "little" choices represents a choice between right and wrong. Every decision represents an opportunity to select either God's will or your own way. *Consider the choice* means to stop and ask yourself, "Who determines what is right or wrong in this situation?" It should help you remember that your choice is not between what *you think* is right and wrong; it's between what is objectively right and wrong regardless of what you think.

C2. *Compare it to God.* Compare your choice of action to the nature and character of God. First, compare your choice to God's *precepts*— the rules, regulations, codes, and requirements of Scripture. Are there specific Bible passages that tell you what to do in this instance?

Second, compare your choice to a universal *principle* based on Scripture. Principles help explain the "why" behind the precepts.

For example, the basic principle behind the Ten Commandment precept "You shall not give false testimony" (Exod. 20:16) is honesty. The principle behind "You shall not murder" (Exod. 20:13) is love. Is there a scriptural principle that applies to the choice you need to make?

Third, compare your choice to the *person* of God. The precepts and principles of Scripture ultimately point us to God. Moses prayed, "If you are pleased with me, teach me your ways so I may know you" (Exod. 33:13). Moses recognized that learning God's ways—understanding His precepts and the principles behind them—would help him grow to know the person of God Himself. When you compare a specific choice or course of action to God, you will begin to see the will of God more clearly.

C3. *Commit to God's way.* Once you have compared your selfish desires to God's absolute standard, you must choose between your way and God's way. Nobody can do this for you. You must consciously turn from your selfish way and firmly commit to God's way.

C4. *Count on God's protection and provision.* When you admit God's sovereignty and submit to His loving authority, you can begin to count on His protection and provision. This doesn't mean everything will be rosy. In fact, God says pretty bluntly that you may suffer at times for choosing to live by His standard of righteousness. But living God's way brings many spiritual blessings, like freedom from guilt, a clear conscience, the joy of sharing Christ, and, most important, the blessing of God on your life. You may also enjoy many physical, emotional, psychological, and relational benefits when you commit to God's ways. While God's protection and provision should not be the primary motivation for obeying Him, it certainly provides powerful encouragement for choosing His will.

"So once I am committed to following God's universal will," you may say, "how do I discover

God's specific will day by day?" Seeking His will is done most effectively through the four-step process Jenny explained to Ashley.

Seek God's will in the Bible. Knowing Scripture is basic to seeking and understanding God's will. For example, you don't have to wonder whether God wants you to marry an unbeliever, because 2 Corinthians 6:14 states, "Do not be yoked together with unbelievers. For what do righteousness and wickedness have in common? Or what fellowship can light have with darkness?" If your idea of God's specific will for you doesn't line up with Scripture, then it's your will, not God's.

Seek God's will in prayer. Jesus taught His disciples to pray, "Our Father in heaven, hallowed be your name, your kingdom come, your will be done on earth as it is in heaven" (Matt. 6:9–10). God is not hiding His will from you; He is willing and able to give you the direction you seek. Ask Him for it daily and as often as you need to.

Seek God's will in the counsel of others. God has placed wise, mature Christians in your life to help you discern God's specific will. Your parents, grandparents, or other family members may fill this role. You may also receive helpful guidance from your youth leader, your Sunday-school teacher, and your minister. The counsel of wise Christian adults will help you in a couple of ways. First, seeking the objective opinion of others may keep you from making an emotional decision on your own. Second, a mature believer can speak from a background of experiences you may not have.

Seek God's will in your circumstances. God often directs us through external circumstances that are seemingly beyond our control. For example, you may have a special aptitude for music and be offered a generous scholarship to study music at the university. These circumstances may seem to point toward getting a music degree, so you cannot ignore them. On the other hand, suppose you are interested in pursuing a profession or ministry centering on your music ability, but you are unable to get a scholarship and you have no resources for college. Just because circumstances seem to be against you does not mean a music career is not in God's specific will for your life. The circumstances in your life alone do not always clearly indicate God's will. Circumstances must be balanced by Scripture, prayer, and the wise counsel of others. Let's assume that you are conforming your life to God's universal will (salvation, submission, life in the Spirit, etc.) and you have sought His specific will in Scripture, prayer, counsel, and circumstances. How do you decide what to do? Simply *do what you want to do*. Psalm 37:4 promises, "Delight yourself in the LORD and he will give you the desires of your heart." As you conform to God's universal will and seek His specific will, you are free to follow the desires of your heart. Since you are delighting in the Lord and in His will, you are free to walk by faith, believing that if your desires are somehow not in God's will, He will make it clear to you.

As you seek to determine God's will in the important decisions of your life, you are blessed if you have trusted Christian friends to pray with you and talk with you, as Bobby and Ashley have discovered.

Bobby's and Ashley's Story

As soon as Bobby arrived home from the back-packing trip Sunday afternoon, he called Ashley. He had missed her during his three days away and hoped they could spend some time together. Ashley had missed Bobby, too, and was waiting for his call. It was such a warm day, they decided to meet at the county park, which had a large garden full of blooming flowers. Bobby said he would bring his camera, which he had taken on the back-packing trip. He wanted to take some pictures to use up the last few exposures on the roll.

Strolling hand in hand through the garden, they talked about their respective weekend activities. Bobby described the fish he'd caught and the great time he'd had with Doug Shaw and his three senior friends. Ashley shared the details of the sleepover at Jenny's, the makeovers, and the shopping trip. Neither mentioned the deep conversations that had occurred with their friends.

Ashley was about to bring up the topic when Bobby said, "Sitting around the campfire, we had some good, long talks."

"About baseball and fishing, I suppose," Ashley joked.

Bobby laughed. "Yeah, that too. But I mean some serious stuff, like talking about God's will for our lives. We asked Doug about his background, how God led him to do what he's doing. It was real interesting. We even had a good prayer time about God's will for our lives."

Ashley's eyes widened. "That's too weird. We talked about God's will, too, and had a time of prayer. We bugged Jenny to tell us her story." Ashley was careful not to mention her specific interest in how Jenny and Doug had chosen each other.

Comparing notes, they laughed about how similar their "serious talks" had been. Bobby related Doug's story of serving in the navy to earn money for college, then working for his father until he could save enough for his own business. Ashley shared a little about Jenny's story, carefully downplaying the dating and marriage elements. She and Bobby agreed that Doug and Jenny Shaw were a wealth of information about God's universal will and specific

will, and that their lives were a good example of
both.

A patch of jonquils and daffodils in full
bloom diverted their attention for a few minutes.
Bobby took several pictures of Jenny standing
among the beautiful flowers. For the final expo-
sure on the roll, he asked a passerby to snap their
picture together.

As they resumed their walk, Ashley gathered
her courage to ask the question she had timidly
avoided all year. "So what do you think God's
specific will is for your life, Bobby—I mean
about college and baseball and stuff?" She realized that the "stuff" she was referring to was
her.

"I've been thinking about that a lot lately,
you know, with graduation just a few weeks away.
Everybody has been bugging me for a decision
about college and baseball."

"You've been really busy playing baseball and
getting ready for finals," Ashley rationalized for
him. "Plus, you're head of the leadership team for
the youth group."

"Yeah, I've been busy," Bobby agreed, "but

that's not why I haven't made any big decisions yet."

Ashley waited. She knew Bobby would tell her more when he was ready.

"Actually, I've been a little slow because I wasn't real sure how to find out what God wants me to do. This weekend with Doug really helped. I have a much better idea what the Bible says about seeking God's will."

"Yes, me too," Ashley said. Then she waited silently as they walked.

Bobby motioned to a bench along the path and they sat down. He joked about needing to rest after hiking almost twenty miles during the weekend.

"I realize that there are three things that are important to me right now," Bobby said as they faced each other on the bench. "First is God. Second is you—us, really, and our future. Third is baseball. During high school they all fit together pretty well. Now I have to make some choices, and I've been waiting for God to tell me what to do. But after this weekend I realize that He expects me to be involved in the process."

"Funny, but that's what I've been thinking since the sleepover," Ashley put in. "Even though my parents and I agree that I should go to State, I'm not sure what my major should be. It was a real revelation to know that God allows room for us to make some choices."

"As long as we are committed to obeying God's universal will and seeking His specific will," Bobby added, remembering Doug's comments.

"Right," Ashley affirmed. Then her question tumbled out before she could stop it: "So what do you *want* to do, Bobby?" Then she held her breath.

Bobby surveyed the sky as he thought. Finally he said, "Well, I don't feel called to the ministry right now, so Bible college is not a high priority to me at this point. Some day I might want to take some classes there, but not right now."

"Mm," Ashley responded. She was quietly pleased that one option for taking Bobby out of the area had apparently been crossed off his list.

"As for turning pro," Bobby continued, "I don't think I'm ready. Players at my level spend years in the minor leagues separated from their families and living out of a suitcase. I would be better off playing college baseball and getting a degree at the same time. In four years, if the scouts are still interested in me, I can make a decision about professional baseball."

Ashley smiled inside. So far Bobby wanted the same things she wanted. "Where would you like to go to college?" she probed. "You have a few scholarship offers to choose from."

Bobby nodded. "This is where the other priorities in my life have helped me see what I want more clearly. I really hope to do some kind of part-time volunteer ministry during college, and Doug has asked me to serve as a youth ministry intern next year if I'm still around. It sounds like a perfect fit to me." Bobby reached over to take Ashley's hand. "Besides, being away from you is definitely not what I want. I could do it if God directed me to. But this weekend I realized that God is pleased to give me the desires of my heart. And my heart's desire is to be with you."

Ashley gripped Bobby's hand as tears of joy filled her eyes. Bobby continued, "I don't know what the long-term future holds for us, Ashley. Like Doug and Jenny say, God usually reveals His will a day at a time. But I want our immediate futures to be together. State has a decent baseball program, and they have offered me a modest scholarship. So for now at least, I want to go to school with you at State—if that's what you want."

Tears cascaded down Ashley's cheeks. "More than anything, I want God's will for both of us," she said. "And if His will is to give me the desires of my heart, I couldn't be happier with your decision."

Bobby and Ashley talked for an hour about their dreams for the future. Then, hand in hand, they spent several minutes committing their dreams and desires to God in prayer. After a long, joyful embrace, they headed off for the local Mexican fast-food restaurant. They laughed as they agreed that tacos and burritos were definitely in God's will for them this evening.

Time Out to Consider

It's too soon to tell if Bobby will play professional baseball or if he and Ashley will eventually be

married. But their concerns about these important decisions have already begun to diminish.
They have some definite, biblical guidelines for
seeking God's will for their lives, and they are
committed to following those guidelines. You can
enjoy the same confidence about finding God's
will as you apply these basic principles to your
life.

Be conformed to the universal will of God.
Make it your goal to obey God's revealed will
concerning salvation—living in the Spirit, sharing your faith, obeying your parents, remaining
sexually pure, and so on.

Be informed about the specific will of God.
Submit every decision to the four-step process of
Scripture, prayer, counsel, and circumstances.

Submit to the revealed will of God. Cultivate a
daily walk of faith, believing that if your desires
are not God's will, He will let you know.

Do what you want. Live with confidence that
God will give you the desires of your heart as
long as your number one desire is to serve Him.

Don't worry about the future. God is sover-
eign and your future is in His hands, so don't

worry about marriage or your career. Simply say daily, "Lord, I want to do what You want." Then it is up to Him to work in you to accomplish His will and fulfill your desires.

APPENDIX

Several times in this book I have mentioned the work of Dr. David Ferguson. David's ministry has had such a profound effect on me in the past several years that I want you to have every opportunity to be exposed to his work and ministry. David and his wife, Teresa, direct a ministry called Intimate Life Ministries.

WHO AND WHAT IS INTIMATE LIFE MINISTRIES?

Intimate Life Ministries (ILM) is a training and resource ministry whose purpose is to *assist in the development of Great Commandment ministries worldwide.* Great Commandment ministries—ministries that help us love God and our neighbors—are ongoing ministries that deepen

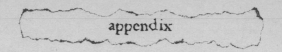

our intimacy with God and with others in marriage, family, and the church.

Intimate Life Ministries comprises:

- A network of **churches** seeking to fortify homes and communities with God's love;

- A network of **pastors and other ministry leaders** walking intimately with God and their families and seeking to live vulnerably before their people;

- A team of **accredited trainers** committed to helping churches establish ongoing Great Commandment ministries;

- A team of **professional associates** from ministry and other professional Christian backgrounds, assisting with research, training, and resource development;

- **Christian broadcasters, publishers, media, and other affiliates,** cooperating to see marriages and families reclaimed as divine relationships;

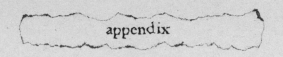

- **Headquarters staff** providing strategic planning, coordination, and support.

HOW CAN INTIMATE LIFE MINISTRIES SERVE YOU?
ILM's Intimate Life Network of Churches is an effective, ongoing support and equipping relationship with churches and Christian leaders. There are at least four ways ILM can serve you:

1. *Ministering to Ministry Leaders*
ILM offers a unique two-day "Galatians 6:6" retreat to ministers and their spouses for personal renewal and for reestablishing and affirming ministry and family priorities. The conference accommodations and meals are provided as a gift to ministry leaders by cosponsoring partners. Thirty to forty such retreats are held throughout the U.S. and Europe each year.

2. *Partnering with Denominations and Other Ministries*
Numerous denominations and ministries have partnered with ILM by "commissioning" them to equip their ministry leaders through the Galatians

6:6 retreats along with strategic training and ongoing resources. This unique partnership enables a denomination to use the expertise of ILM trainers and resources to perpetuate a movement of Great Commandment ministry at the local level. ILM also provides a crisis-support setting to which denominations may send ministers, couples, or families who are struggling in their relationships.

3. *Identifying, Training, and Equipping Lay Leaders*

ILM is committed to helping the church equip its lay leaders through:

- *Sermon Series* on several Great Commandment topics to help pastors communicate a vision for Great Commandment health as well as identify and cultivate a core lay leadership group.

- *Community Training Classes* that provide weekly or weekend training to church staff and lay leaders. Classes are delivered by Intimate

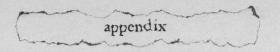

Life trainers along with ILM video-assisted training, workbooks, and study courses.

• *One-Day Training Conferences* on implementing Great Commandment ministry in the local church through marriage, parenting, or singles ministry. Conducted by Intimate Life trainers, these conferences are a great way to jump-start Great Commandment ministry in a local church.

4. *Providing Advanced Training and Crisis Support*

ILM conducts advanced training for both ministry staff and lay leaders through the Leadership Institute, focusing on relational ministry (marriage, parenting, families, singles, men, women, blended families, and counseling). The Enrichment Center provides support to relationships in crisis through Intensive Retreats for couples, families, and singles.

For more information on how you, your church, or your denomination can take advantage of the many services and resources, such as

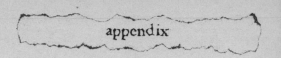

the Great Commandment Ministry Training
Resource offered by Intimate Life Ministries,
write or call:

Intimate Life Ministries
P.O. Box 201808
Austin, TX 78720-1808
1-800-881-8008
www.ilmministries.com

Connecting Youth in Crisis

Obtain other vital topics from the PROJECT 911 Collection...

Experience the Connection

For Youth & Youth Groups

This eight-week youth group experience will teach your youth the true meaning of deepened friendships—being a 911 friend. Each lesson is built upon scriptural teachings that will both bond your group together and serve to draw others to Christ.

This optional video is an excellent supplement to your group's workbook experience.

As follow-up to your youth group experience, continue a young person's friendship journey by introducing them to a thirty-day topical devotional journal and a book on discovering God's will in their life.

Experience the Connection

For Adults & Groups

Book on Audio

This watershed book is for parents, pastors, youth workers, or anyone interested in seeing youth not only survive but thrive in today's culture.

THE FATHER CONNECTION

This book, directed specifically to fathers, offers ten qualities to form deepened relationships between dads and their kids.

Begin your church-wide emphasis with an adult group experience using this five-part video series. Josh provides biblical insights for relationally connecting with your youth.

Experience the Connection

For Youth Workers

A one-on-one resource to help you provide a relational response and spiritual guidance to the 24 most troubling issues youth face today.

This handbook brings together over forty youth specialists to share their insights on what makes a successful youth ministry.

Contact your Christian supplier to obtain these PROJECT 911 resources and begin experiencing the connection God intended.

ABOUT THE AUTHORS

JOSH MCDOWELL, internationally known speaker, author, and traveling representative of Campus Crusade for Christ, International, has authored or coauthored more than fifty books, including *Right from Wrong* and *Josh McDowell's Handbook on Counseling Youth*. Josh and his wife, Dottie, have four children and live in Dallas, Texas.

ED STEWART is the author or coauthor of numerous Christian books. A veteran writer, Ed Stewart began writing fiction for youth as a coauthor with Josh McDowell. He has since authored four suspense novels for adults. Ed and his wife, Carol, live in Hillsboro, Oregon. They have two grown children and four grandchildren.